MW00579844

IMAGES
of America

ENCINO

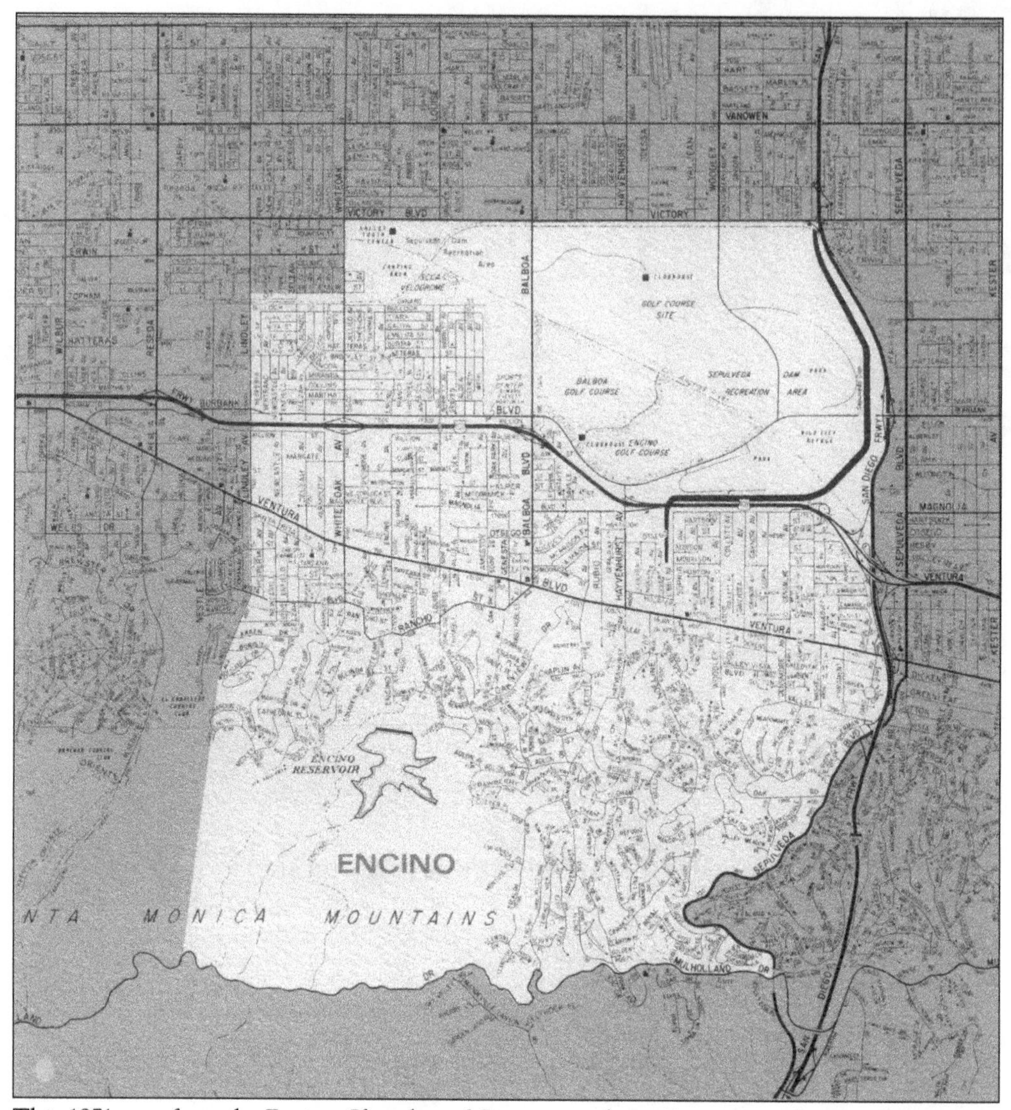

This 1971 map from the Encino Chamber of Commerce shows Encino as a district of the city of Los Angeles located in the central portion of the southern San Fernando Valley. It derives its name from the Rancho Los Encinos (Ranch of the Oaks), an 1845 Mexican land grant of 4,468 acres to three Mission Indians following the closing of the California missions in the 1800s. Encino is bordered by Tarzana (Lindley Avenue) on the west, Van Nuys (Victory Boulevard) on the north, Sherman Oaks (the San Diego Freeway and Sepulveda Boulevard) on the east, and Mulholland Drive on the south. (Courtesy of Los Encinos Archives.)

ON THE COVER: Happy days are here at the dedication of the first Encino Post Office in 1938. Some of Encino's celebrities are in the picture. Holding a white hat is the honorary mayor, Al Jolson. The man holding the flag is actor Edward Everett Horton. To the right of the flag is Peter Amestoy. Other proud Encino residents are Phil Harris, Don Ameche, Arthur Treacher, and race car driver Barney Oldfield. (Courtesy of Ted Gibson.)

Michael Crosby

ISBN 978-1-5316-4589-2

Published by Arcadia Publishing
Charleston, South Carolina

Library of Congress Control Number: 2008935193

For all general information contact Arcadia Publishing at:
Telephone 843-853-2070
Fax 843-853-0044
E-mail sales@arcadiapublishing.com
For customer service and orders:
Toll-Free 1-888-313-2665

Visit us on the Internet at www.arcadiapublishing.com

Contents

ACKNOWLEDGMENTS

This book is comprised, for the most part, of the photographs from the Los Encinos Archives (unless otherwise noted). The archive was created after the 1994 Northridge Earthquake caused major structural damage to all the historic buildings at Los Encinos State Historic Park. The California Department of Parks and Recreation needed to have an organized collection of all the historical information so they could accurately restore the buildings. A special acknowledgment goes to Jim Newland, Nancy Mendez, and Alexa Clauson. They and the entire staff of historians and conservators deserve the greatest recognition for their wonderful work.

Walter Nelson deserves thanks for keeping the activities going with his living history programs as a past president of the docent association. Special thanks go to Lil Baur, who has served the park for many years with the historical society and the docent association. Her historical knowledge, support, and friendship are greatly appreciated and cherished. And I have to mention my deep appreciation to the devoted volunteers and their families who have given so much of their time to Los Encinos.

Encino is a relatively new community in the valley. Collecting the needed number of photographs that describe the growth of the community was difficult. There is no central library. Marc Wanamaker and the Bison Archives provided amazing photographs of the RKO Ranch and early activities on Ventura Boulevard. Claude Zachary and the University of Southern California Special Collections helped fill the gaps.

I could not have finished this book without the loving and meticulous help of Amy Goldenberg. She is a talented artist and woman of letters whose attention to detail made her a worthy companion as we tracked down the facts of history.

I appreciate all the volunteer family members and photographers who have donated their pictures to Los Encinos State Historic Park. However, most valuable is the dedication of the many volunteers who have spent countless hours of their time to keep the history and culture of California alive for future generations.

INTRODUCTION

On the afternoon of August 5, 1769, Spanish captain Gaspar de Portola led an expedition of 64 men and 100 mules up the California coast to find the fabled Monterey Bay. Blocked by steep cliffs at the shore of Santa Monica Bay, they traveled up a Native American trail through a canyon known today as the Sepulveda Pass in the Santa Monica Mountains and happened upon a vast valley of tall grass and scattered groves of oaks, or *encinos*, and a gentle river lined with reeds. They named the place El Valle de Santa Catalina de Bononia de los Encinos. At an artesian spring in the area of today's Encino, they met a society of native people. Fr. Juan Crespi, the expedition's diarist, mentions the spring and tribal area in his writings of the expedition. He wrote, "Two large villages of very fine, well-behaved and very friendly heathens who must have amounted to about 200 souls, men, women and children. They offered us their seeds in baskets." In a 1980s archaeological dig of the area that was dubbed "The Lost Village of Encino," old Spanish beads were unearthed.

The modern city of Encino began around this artesian spring that served as a gathering place of many tribes, including the Tataviam, Chumash, and Tongva, for several thousand years. This ancient spring still provides water today within the grounds of Los Encinos State Historic Park, a tiny jewel hidden along the busy Ventura Boulevard. In the early 1800s, with the development of the mission system, native tribes were merged together into the Mission San Fernando del Rey and called the *Fernandenos* by the Spanish. With the breakdown of the mission system in 1834, native peoples homesteaded the land surrounding the spring.

On July 8, 1845, Gov. Pio Pico officially recognized the claim of three Mission Indians named Roman, Francisco, and Roque. They were given a 4,460-acre rancho (1 Mexican league) in what was to become Rancho El Encino. The families grazed cattle and horses while growing simple crops with the help of the spring and the gentle river.

The heirs to the land grant lost ownership in the late 1840s because of a variety of financial disputes. Over the next several decades, there was an interesting, and at times controversial, international sequence of ownership of the rancho from Californio, French, Basque, and American owners. The de la Ossa family, the Thompsons, the Garniers, the Oxararts, the Glesses, and the Amestoys all owned the rancho land, each owner making his mark on its development in some way. Most significantly, Vicente de la Ossa, the first owner after Native American occupancy, built the adobe in 1849 to house his large family and service the travelers along El Camino Real. French brothers Eugene and Phillipe Garnier built the two-story limestone building in 1872. Over the following years, both structures have withstood neglect, urbanization, and the threat of demolition, not to mention serious earthquake damage. Yet the buildings still stand to this day.

In 1915, when property values skyrocketed and other communities in the San Fernando Valley began spreading out, the Amestoy family began selling off portions of their rancho for the future community of Encino. However, the area remained largely rural and sparsely populated through the late 1930s. Maps and aerial photographs of the San Fernando Valley from the time show the area of Encino as still fairly undeveloped. The Army Corps of Engineers bought several hundred acres at the northern end of the old rancho following the devastating flood of 1938. They built the iconic Sepulveda Dam in the flood basin and created a cement channel for the erratic Los Angeles River.

In the post–World War II boom, the community began to grow along Ventura Highway, and movie stars like Clark Gable, Mickey Rooney, and Al Jolson built large homes in the Encino hills south of what is now Ventura Boulevard. The rich and famous still live in the lush hillside above the old rancho.

In 1945, the last remaining four acres of Rancho El Encino were going on the market, and the old adobe and two-story limestone building were slated for demolition. Encino resident Marie Stewart and the Encino Women's Club roused support and saved the historical monument from the fate of so many other Los Angeles landmarks. In 1949, the 100-year-old adobe, with the remaining land and structures, became officially incorporated as part of the California State Park System. Los Encinos State Historic Park sits on the corner of Ventura Boulevard and La Maida Avenue, an oasis of beauty and history in the midst of a busy and ever-growing city.

One

THE LAND OF THE CALIFORNIOS

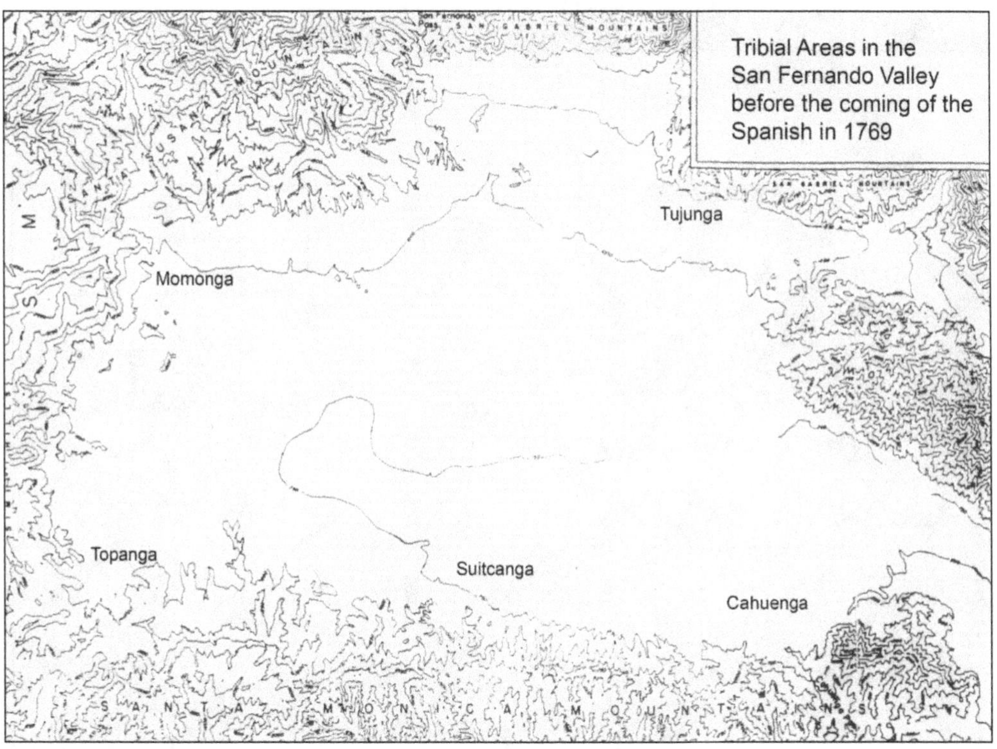

This tribal map shows Shoshone and Chumash *ranchorias*, or villages, that populated the semiarid San Fernando Valley before the Spanish arrived in 1769. The native people utilized the freshwater springs and streams along with other abundant resources of the fertile San Fernando Valley. They had been living there for the past 4,000 years. The Tataviam, Chumash, and Tongva Indian tribes lived together along the hillside of the valley. Suitcanga (Encino), Kawengna (Cahuenga), Topanga, Momonga (Chatsworth), and Tujunga were the various village names found on the San Fernando Mission registers. The Chumash territory spread from present-day Malibu and Topanga to southern Monterey County. The Tataviam people settled in the Santa Clarita Valley. Tataviam roughly translates to "People of the southern slopes." The Tongva people occupied the area around Los Angeles and the San Gabriel Valley. The native Tongva used the "nga" sound to denote place names.

Gaspar de Portola led an expedition over the Sepulveda Pass on August 5, 1769. Father Crespi wrote, "We saw a very pleasant and spacious valley. We descended to it and stopped close to a watering place, which is a large pool. Near it we found a village of heathen, very friendly and docile. We gave to this plain the name of Santa Catalina de Bononia de Los Encinos."

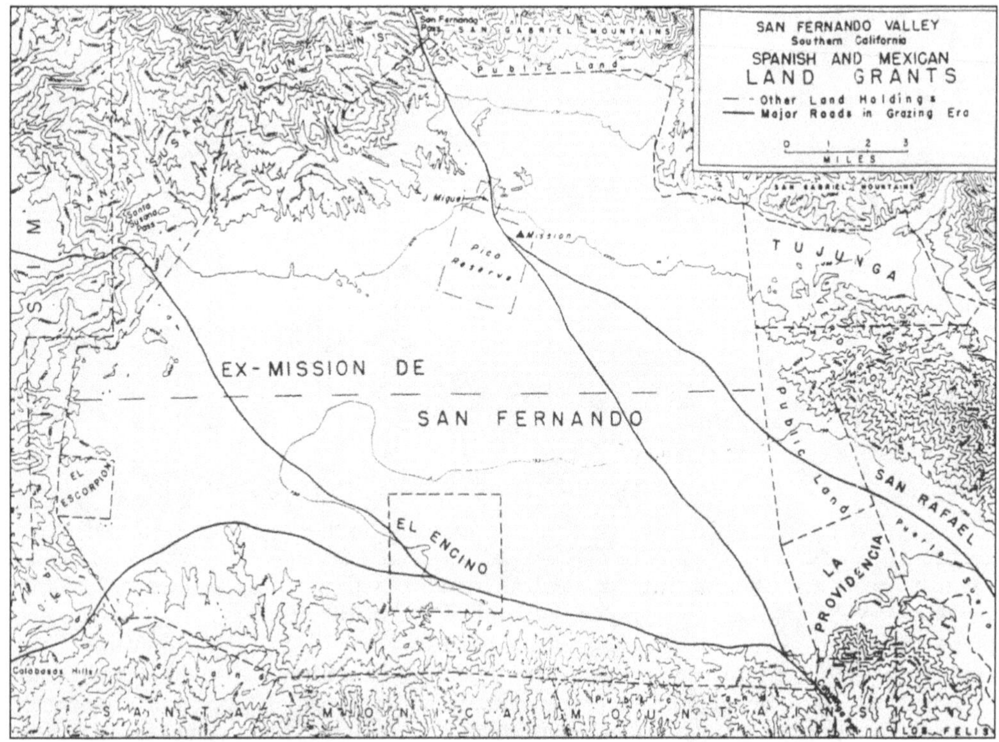

Mission San Fernando Rey de España was founded in 1797 on the site of the Pashecgna village but closed following Mexico's Secularization Laws of 1834. At its peak, the mission had 30,000 grapevines, winemaking facilities, and 21,000 head of cattle. The valley holdings were divided up into the five land grants of El Escorpion, El Encino, El Providencia, the Pico Reserve, and the ex–Mission San Fernando.

Antonio Ortega's great-grandfather Tiburcio Cayo, originally from the Taapu Village in the Santa Clarita Valley, spent most of his life in service at the San Fernando Mission. When the mission system dissolved, he homesteaded the land around the Encino spring in 1838. In 1840, a license was granted to Tiburcio. After Tiburcio's death, Mexican governor Pio Pico formally granted El Encino to Roman, Francisco, and Roque on July 18, 1845. But as family members began to die, the ranch could not be maintained, and taxes fell behind; they were forced to sell the ranch. Tiburcio's wife, Teresa, and their two daughters, Paula and Aquida, continued to live on the rancho. Rita, the daughter of Paula and Francisco, gave birth to Antonio Ortega on the rancho in 1849. (Courtesy of Beverly Folkes.)

This panoramic view of the Encino hay field in 1915 offers a glimpse of what the valley might have looked like before it became urbanized. In order to see what Encino looked like 100 years ago, one has to remove all the houses and streets, all the office buildings and shopping malls, and leave only scattered groves of oak trees and an empty plain. The mission brought cattle and horse ranching into the valley, followed by the sheep industry of the 1870s. When the wool market fell,

dry crops such as wheat and barley were grown. Eventually, as smaller farms sprang up with the import of Owens Valley water in 1913, other crops included alfalfa, apricots, asparagus, barley hay, beans, beets, cabbage, citrus, corn, lettuce, melons, peaches, potatoes, pumpkins, squash, tomatoes, and walnuts. But valley agriculture slowly died after the end of World War II.

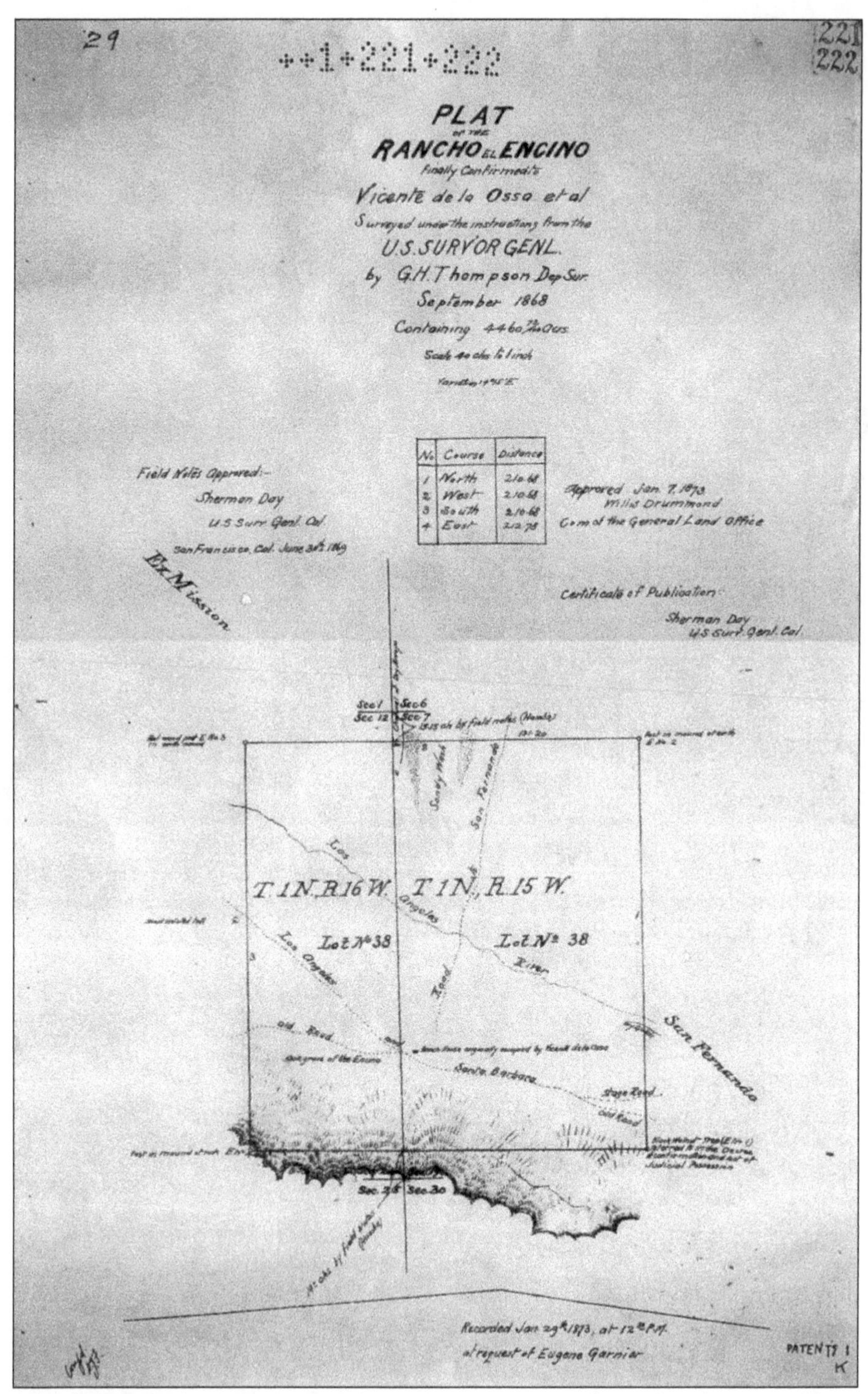

This official plat map drawn up for Frenchman Eugene Garnier shows that the original boundary of the Encino Rancho land grant included 4,460 acres. Today's boundaries correspond with what is now White Oak Boulevard from Haynes Street, south to the Encino Reservoir, east to Firmament Avenue near Sutton Street, north to Haynes Street, and then back to White Oak.

Vicente de la Ossa purchased the land around the spring from the Ortega family and built a nine-room adobe in 1849 at the intersection of the old El Camino Real and San Fernando Mission roads. Here he raised cattle and operated a roadhouse for travelers, and in the March 18, 1859, issue of the *L.A. Star* newspaper, de la Ossa announced, "I have established a place for the purpose of affording accommodations to the people traveling on this road. They will find, at all times, food for themselves and for the horses, and bed at night."

Jose Vicente de los Reyes de la Ossa was baptized on January 6, 1808, born to a military family at the Presidio of San Diego. In 1842, he received the grant Rancho Providencia (Burbank). Vicente and Rita de la Ossa owned the ranch from 1849 until 1862. According to land case records, de la Ossa had "looked out" for the Native Americans who owned Encino prior to him in exchange for the right to purchase the rancho from them.

Rita Guillen was born on May 21, 1817, in San Diego. Rita's father, Miguel Antonio Guillen, a soldier at the Presidio, died when she was two years old. Her mother, Eulalia Perez de Guillen Marine, moved to the San Gabriel Mission, where she became the "keeper of the keys." Rita married Vicente in Los Angeles in June 1832. He was 24 years old and she was 15.

De la Ossa's rancho wine was famous. In pursuit of Native Americans in 1853, Horace Bell and his posse arrived at Encino: "We drew up in martial array before the hospitable castle of the lordly Don Vicente de la Ossa, the baronial proprietor of the Rancho del Encino, who cordially invited us to dismount, stake our jaded mustangs and refresh the inner man." (Photograph by Amy Goldenberg.)

De la Ossa captured spring water for a reservoir, pictured in this 1901 photograph. He noted, "Being desirous of changing my residence, I offer for sale my rancho, known as El Encino containing three miles square, situated 18½ miles from Los Angeles. There is on the rancho an abundance of grass, and timber of all kinds, is watered by springs, both cold and warm, the latter possessing medicinal qualities."

Maria Manuela, the oldest of 13 children, was born in 1833. Her godparents were Gov. Pio Pico and Catalina Verdugo. The rest of Rita's children were Susana, born in 1835; Antonio, 1838; Fabricio, 1840; Constancia, 1842; Vicente, 1843; Pablo, 1845; Clotilde, 1849; David, birth date unknown; Leonora, birth date unknown; Maclovia, birth date unknown; Carlos II, 1859; and Florestina, 1862.

James P. Thompson, known as "Don Santiago," was born in New Hampshire and died on May 12, 1895, at 74 years of age. His career included sheriff, road builder, sheep rancher, and jail warden. Thompson was an experienced ranchero when he obtained a five-year lease to half of Rancho La Brea in 1852. The adobe occupied by Thompson still stands near the Farmers Market at Third Street and Fairfax Avenue in Los Angeles.

Manuela married Thompson in March 1851 and came to live at the rancho after 1860. His mother-in-law, the widowed Rita de la Ossa, conveyed to him Rancho El Encino, where they continued to live, on September 10, 1862. But Manuela died in 1868, leaving children of ages 10, 7, and 6. Thompson sold the ranch the following year and remarried. Several lawsuits were filed over the division of the ranch between Rita and Thompson. There is no doubt all of this action put great hardship and strain on the family.

The de la Ossa sisters pictured here in the fashionable attire of the 1890s are, from left to right, (first row) Susana, Maclovia (or Lola), and Florestina; (second row) Constancia and Clotilde. The de la Ossa family spoke Spanish, and the children learned English in school. For the stylish de la Ossa daughters, household chores of cooking, baking, and sewing were a daily routine. The older children spent the weekdays in Los Angeles to attend school. In 1856, Vicente Jr. attended Santa Clara College in San Jose. The children were baptized at the Plaza Church in Los Angeles or at the Mission San Gabriel.

Marguerita Amelia de la Ossa wears a very stylish hat in this dawn-of-the-20th-century photograph. Born in 1880, she was the daughter of Jose Vicente II and granddaughter of Vicente de la Ossa. She married Charles Edward Eichelberger and gave birth to two boys: William and Charles.

The lovely Florestina de la Ossa (top center), the youngest of the family, strikes a pose in her athletic clothes with her school friends, the Temple daughters. Florestina was known for her long beautiful hair.

Now a young lady, Florestina de la Ossa is dressed in fashionable attire from around 1890. Her father, Vicente, died on July 20, 1861, at the age of 53 when her mother, Rita, was pregnant with Florestina, their 13th child.

This hand-tinted photographic print of Florestina de la Ossa was made around 1925. She was active for many years in the Native Daughters of the Golden West. One of her proudest moments was when the Vicente de la Ossa Adobe was set aside as a Southern California historic landmark by the Los Angeles chapter of the organization in 1950.

Florestina married Harlow Gilbert in San Gabriel in 1887. Gilbert operated a marble and stone business for many years in Los Angeles. He died in 1920. They had two children: Inez and Vernor. Inez later married Roger O'Shea.

The large de la Ossa clan would gather each year for family reunions, such as this one from the 1900s. The de la Ossas, along with the other rancho families, still feel connected to Encino and their heritage. They often visit the old adobe at Los Encinos State Historic Park. All of the families connected to the property return to reconnect to their past and share family stories.

Two

The French Influence

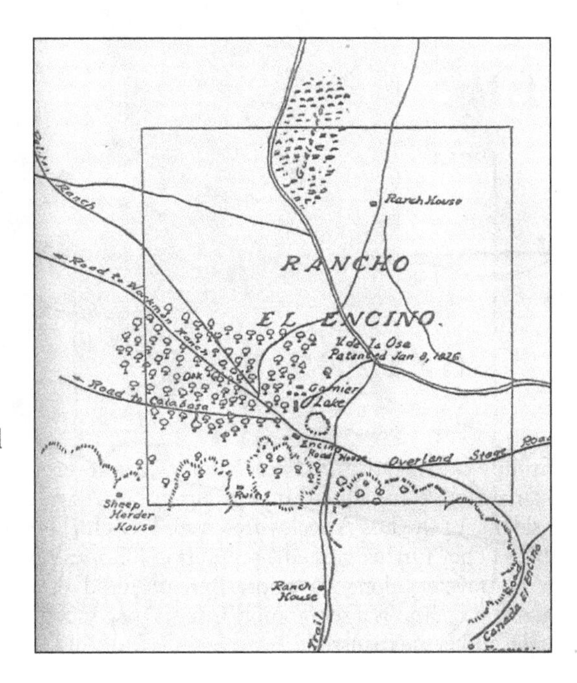

Eugene Garnier and his brothers purchased Rancho El Encino in 1868, shortly after the death of Manuela Thompson. This map of Garnier's ranch in 1874 marks the "Encino Road House" as well as the cluster of buildings around the pond. On the north side of the ranch, a "Ranch House" is marked, and several major roads cross through the land. The Garniers are credited for many improvements to the ranch. They erected a two-story limestone house using materials from a local quarry. It contained sleeping quarters on the second floor, a dining room, a kitchen, and a bakery. The lake was lined with the same limestone into the shape of a Spanish guitar. A pitched, wooden roof was also added to the adobe. They expanded the hospitality service of the ranch by adding a cluster of buildings around the pond.

Phillipe Garnier, pictured here, along with his brothers Eugene, Camille, and Leon, was part of a large, active French cultural group in Los Angeles. The 1860 U.S. Census recorded that 200 residents of the Los Angeles area were French. The Garniers were well-known wool men in the 1870s. They further gained a reputation for offering excellent meals at Rancho El Encino to the many travelers along the Santa Barbara Road. A visitor to the rancho during this time wrote, "On the Encino is a remarkably fine spring, which flows a number of thousand gallons of water daily, and is inexhaustible."

In 1874, future San Fernando Valley ranch owner Benjamin F. Porter stayed all night as the guest of Gen. Andres Pico, who was then living at Mission San Fernando. The next morning, Porter drove with the general and Charles Maclay to the Encino Rancho for breakfast, a distance of 15 miles. Porter recalled, "This was another large ranch on the west side of the Valley and owned by the Garnier brothers, two Frenchmen. The food at this ranch was famous, so the General always made it a part of his entertainment to drive his guest there for a meal."

These two photographs, donated by visiting Garnier descendants to Los Encinos State Historic Park in the late 1980s, show the two-story European home of the Garnier family, a replica of the Encino structure, which had been built first. It is situated in the town of Gap, in the St. Leger region at the base of the French Alps. Gap is the capital of the Hautes-Alpes Department, or state, and is the largest town in the Southern Alps. It was first inhabited in 14 AD by the Romans, who recognized the importance of its strategic position linking Turin, Italy, with the Rhône valley of France. An Alpine crossroads, Gap lies 2,406 feet above sea level on the road to Grenoble. (Both courtesy of the Garnier family.)

In this family portrait from 1893, Phillipe Garnier poses with his wife, Marianne, and their children—from left to right, Pierre, Leon, Albert, and Louise—in their Victorian parlor in Los Angeles. The Garnier brothers, Eugene, Phillipe, Leon, and Camille, were listed in the 1870 U.S. Census as French. Eugene Garnier was deeply in debt to Gaston Oxarart, who filed to evict him from the Encino ranch. Testimony is given that the ranch was mortgaged in September 1875. Further debt followed until the property was foreclosed in November 1877.

Sometime in the 1870s, Phillipe Garnier left Rancho El Encino and started his own ranch. He and brother Camille leased Rancho San Jose de Buenos Ayures (Beverly Hills) for grazing from 1874 to 1881. Phillipe succeeded in business in downtown Los Angeles, where he built and developed the Garnier Block, currently the Chinese American Museum. The building has always been occupied by Chinese tenants since it was built. Phillipe returned to France for health reasons and died in his hometown of Gap in 1898. (Photograph by the author.)

Three

The Basques

Gaston Oxarart was born in the little town of Aldudes, in the French Basque area of the Pyrenees. Oxarart's ownership of Rancho El Encino marked the beginning of a long Basque family history at the site. Oxarart had accumulated considerable wealth by the time of his death on April 23, 1886, when he was 61. In addition to Rancho El Encino, he owned a commercial block in downtown Los Angeles, as well as two vineyards along the east side of the Los Angeles River.

Francisco Oxarart (also known as Frank) was born on July 8, 1873. He was Gaston's son by his common-law wife, Benita. He is pictured here as a young man with his beautiful bride, Julia. Following Gaston Oxarart's death, Frank and his mother were excluded from any inheritance, even as attorneys for Benita tried to prove that Oxarart publicly "recognized, and received and treated Francisco as his legitimate son." Despite this claim, the Oxararts' court actions failed, and the estate was distributed to his nephew, Simon Gless, in 1889.

Frank Oxarart was only 11 years old when his father, Gaston, died. The Gless family buried Gaston in their family plot and paid for Frank to go to college. Frank eventually became an engineer for the Southern Pacific Railroad. He had fond memories of helping his father raise sheep on the Encino ranch.

Simon Francois Gless was born on April 16, 1862, in Copperopolis, California, where his mother managed a hotel. He and his mother came to the Los Angeles area by invitation of his uncle, Gaston Oxarart. Stories tell that Simon blocked anyone from seeing Oxarart in the final weeks of his life. Simon amassed a fortune from his sole inheritance of Gaston's holdings.

Simon married Juanita Amestoy in San Francisco on October 15, 1889, the same year Oxarart's estate was distributed to Gless. Simon appears somewhat uncomfortable sitting in the low chair wearing a fine frock suit, white tie, and gloves in honor of the special day. Juanita wears her beautiful wedding dress with a cascade of flowers down the front.

Juanita Amestoy Gless was born in April 1865 at her father's sheep ranch in Gardena. She was the eldest daughter of Domingo Amestoy and Marie Elizabeth Aycaguer. She came from a large family of five brothers and two sisters.

Juanita is pictured at right in her wedding dress without her veil. Juanita was very proud of her beautiful wedding dress. The dress is one of the highlights of the items and artifacts currently on permanent display at the de la Ossa Adobe at Los Encinos State Historic Park. Visitors are often amazed at Juanita's tiny waist and shoes. Simon and Juanita Gless also pose below in a parlor. Simon is wearing the suit in which he was married, but with a different tie, and Juanita is in a fashionable bustle dress. They are the very model of a comfortable and confident 19th-century American middle-class couple.

Simon and Juanita lived only a short time at the rancho. Shortly afterward, he sold the 4,460-acre Encino Rancho to his father-in-law, Domingo Amestoy, and the Gless family returned to their home in Boyle Heights. Juanita found that her husband was no farmer. He liked the comforts of city life, and in those days, Encino was a day's ride by horse from Los Angeles.

The Gless family poses on their porch in Boyle Heights. Simon stands in the center, while Juanita sits in the chair with Domingo. On the far left stands Theresa Amestoy, Juanita's sister-in-law, with Louise Amestoy, Juanita's sister. Seated on the steps are Joseph Amestoy, Juanita's brother; little Constant Gless; and Elizabeth Amestoy, Juanita's youngest sister. Their maid stands on the porch. Simon died at 41, leaving his wife to raise their three children, Constant, Domingo, and Noeline, who was not yet born at the time of this picture.

Four

The Amestoy Family

Domingo Amestoy and his sons owned the Encino Ranch from 1889 to 1944, longer than any other family. A French Basque, he immigrated to Argentina, and while there, he learned to be a shoemaker. In 1851, he came to Los Angeles, where he began making a living raising sheep. He was worth $1 million at the time of his death in 1892.

The Amestoy family was proud of their Basque heritage, and they often traveled back to Domingo's birthplace of Pinoque, located in the provincial town of St. Pierre d'Irube, in the French Basque Pyrenees. The house where he was born, pictured here, still belongs to Amestoy descendants. Domingo returned to France to marry his sweetheart, Marie Elizabeth Aycaguer, and brought her to America. They had 13 children; eight lived to adulthood.

The children of Domingo and Marie pose for a family portrait taken around 1900. From left to right are (seated) Juanita, Elizabeth, Joseph, Louise, and Jean-Baptiste (or John B.); (standing) Antoine (or Anthony), Michel (or Mike), and Pierre (or Peter). Domingo Amestoy died within a few years of the purchase of the ranch from Gless. After his death, sons Anthony, John B., and Peter operated the ranch.

Young Mike (Michel) Amestoy, born on January 29, 1877, didn't live on the ranch as a child. He and his other siblings stayed in town with family and had a private tutor. On June 22, 1905, he married Elizabeth Munn in New York City and had three children: Michael Jr. on September 10, 1910; John, April 28, 1915; and William, March 19, 1917.

Young Peter loved the ranch. He would spend his summers taking care of the horses, riding in the empty canyons of the Santa Monica Mountains, and roaming the vast grain fields of wheat and barley. At one time, he and his older brothers raised over 3,500 head of sheep.

Peter married Margarite Larre, and they had two children, Genevieve and Simon. The Amestoy brothers made use of large farming machinery, powered by huge teams of horses and steam-powered harvesters. A new rail line was added near the corner of the property, which is now the intersection of Balboa and Victory Boulevards.

Anthony J. Amestoy is shown here in 1894 with his new wife, Theresa Herriott of France. Little is know about Anthony other than the fact that he was one of the older brothers who took over the management of the Amestoy Ranch after Domingo's death. When the sheep market began to no longer be profitable, Anthony and his brothers converted the land to the production of wheat and barley.

Jean-Bapiste, or, as he was known to his English-speaking friends, J. B., married Francoise Hauret from Oloran, a small town in southern France, on October 15, 1893. They had three children: Domingo, Juanita, and Grace. As the eldest of the Amestoy siblings, J. B. was the foreman of the rancho. When he retired, he served as the president of the French Benevolent Society of Los Angeles.

Elizabeth Amestoy Wells, the youngest of Domingo and Marie's children, is pictured here with her son Lawrence in the early 1900s. Elizabeth married Charles W. Wells. They also had another son named Gerald. They lived for many years in Hollywood. Charles died in 1946, and Elizabeth passed away in 1952.

Louise Amestoy, a daughter of Domingo and Marie, was born in France. She married Louis Sentous, who served as the French consul in Los Angeles for 16 years. She was very active in the Franco-American community in Los Angeles until she passed away at her home from heart disease at the age of 58. She was survived by her son, Jean Emile Sentous.

It is chow time for these early-20th-century farmhands, as they take a lunch break during the harvest at the Amestoy Ranch. They are fortunate to be served a hot meal by a renowned Chinese cook, the only standing figure in this photograph.

The Encino spring was used as one of the first mineral springs along El Camino Real. The old bathhouse was a favorite stop for riders along the Butterfield Stage route in the 1880s. They could refresh themselves from the long dusty trip from Los Angeles to San Francisco. The bathhouse fell into disrepair, as shown here with Alex Abel, caretaker of the ranch under the Amestoys, and was later removed.

This 1900 photograph shows the Encino Roadhouse, sometimes called Jake's Tavern. It operated as a stagecoach stop and traveler's inn, as well as a gathering place and job center for Basque immigrants for many years. Built by Eugene Garnier, it was located across State Highway (Ventura Boulevard) from the adobe. Proprietor Jake La Salle, a popular figure in the valley, stands wearing a white coat. The tavern was destroyed by fire in 1906.

The Amestoy family gathers near the aviary outside the adobe in 1901. From left to right are (seated) Joseph Amestoy; Peter Amestoy's daughters, Grace, Juanita, and Genevieve (on her father's knee); Peter Amestoy; Mary Huereta; and Jake La Salle; (standing) Michel Amestoy; Peter Garnier; Michel's wife, Elizabeth; and Francoise and J. B. Amestoy. Sadly, Jake was found dead in 1905 in what appeared to be a suicide.

The cement porch was laid down on the eastern side of the adobe in 1901. This undated photograph shows the old grapevine that used to cover the building. Also visible are the rose bushes planted in front of the porch posts. All the foliage was later removed from the structure by the state in the late 1940s to prevent damage to the old building.

Margarite and Peter Amestoy pose with their children, Genevieve and Simon, along with Buster and Emiline Rambeaud, young cousins of Margarite, in this photograph taken in front of the adobe in the summer of 1906. It is difficult to make out the individual children.

Peter Amestoy and his family lived at the ranch at the beginning of the 20th century. The days of huge harvests of wheat and barley during the years of the late 1800s were coming to an end. A number of the Amestoy family members were no longer interested in sharing the rural lifestyle of the San Fernando Valley. Margarite is shown in this 1906 photograph (left) working on the ranch, where she appears to be butchering a duck while the family dog watches. Peter displays one of his draft horses (below), which were used to pull the harvesters. This was common during the 1890s, for the Amestoys employed 12-horse teams to harvest their rows of wheat. Other photographs in the Los Encinos Archives show Peter with several harness-racing horses.

Pigeons, doves, and jackrabbits were a serious problem for the Amestoy wheat crop. When hunting season opened, many Angelenos came to the hills of Encino in organized hunting parties to help eliminate the trouble. Michel Amestoy is standing on the far left, and Jake La Salle is seated next to him. Jean-Baptiste Amestoy, always fashionable, wears a tie with his shotgun.

Young Simon Amestoy (front center) blows a flute while rancho workers pose with their own instruments. Large vats were kept in the two-story Garnier building containing soy sauce, figs, and apricots. One family story tells that Simon would hide behind the vats and stuff himself while his family searched for him. The Chinese cook, pictured on page 43, who liked the boy, always knew his whereabouts but never tattled on him.

This photograph, taken from the nearby mound south of the lake on the rancho, shows the aviary and garden in front of the adobe and olive trees behind the chicken coop, to the east of the Garnier Building. Runoff from the spring and lake traveled below the white fence in the foreground. The City of Los Angeles eventually routed the runoff into a storm drain that leads to the Los Angeles River.

A man sits in front of the Garnier Building in 1906. The Amestoy Encino Ranch became a company and was incorporated in 1900. The eight Amestoy siblings were all members of the corporation. Peter served as the president and J. B. as ranch manager. They leased portions of the ranch to various enterprises while they still maintained a working farm.

In 1915, brothers Joseph and Antoine Amestoy created the Franco-American Baking Company, located in Boyle Heights. Joseph is pictured, second from the left in the back row, while Antoine (wearing a fedora) stands to the right of a 12-foot-long loaf of bread.

The spring continued to provide water on the rancho property, as shown by the high water level of the lake in this photograph from 1915. The old bathhouse fell into disrepair and neglect. The isolated ranch life in the San Fernando Valley was about to change and begin a transformation into housing subdivisions and other urban developments.

By the 1920s, the old San Fernando Valley mixes with the new in this photograph showing sheep grazing in the field near the adobe, while a new restaurant adds an extension to the two-story Garnier Building. The restaurant operated as a speakeasy during Prohibition, and it was raided several times by the police.

Five

Encino Takes Shape

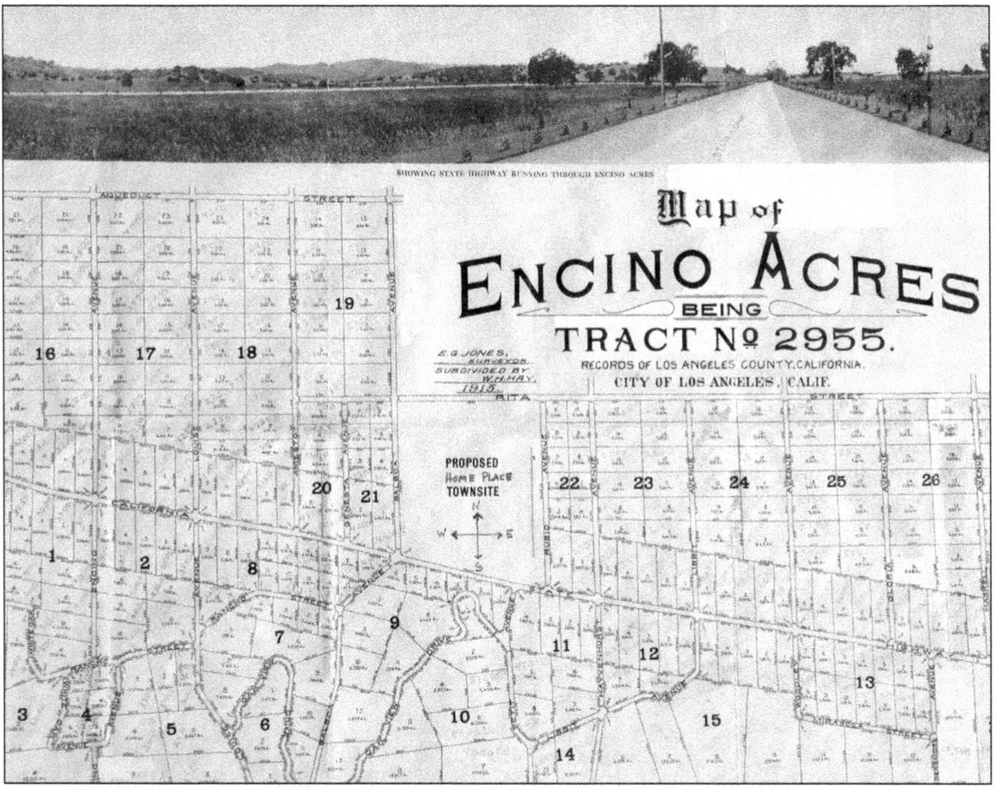

Encino Acres officially opened with an old-fashioned barbecue on April 15, 1916, an event that was the tradition during these years to attract potential buyers to new housing developments. News accounts of this fiesta state that two tons of beef were roasted during an old Spanish-style barbecue. By 10:00 a.m., 200 cars had rolled up to the grove, and by 2:00 p.m., there were 600. San Fernando Valley real estate values began to skyrocket when Henry Mulholland engineered a plan to bring water from the Owens Valley to the citizens of a rapidly expanding population of Los Angeles. William H. Hay, sub-divider and sales agent of Encino Acres, put 200 acres along both sides of the State Highway (Ventura Boulevard) on the market.

William H. Hay, pictured here, purchased land from the Amestoy family for Encino Acres. A considerable portion of the new Encino development was in, or near, the oak-covered foothills of the Santa Monica Mountains. The Amestoys continued to hold much of the area of the Sepulveda Basin for agricultural projects.

This aerial photograph from 1920 shows the barns of the Amestoy Ranch, seen at the middle left. The State Highway (Ventura Boulevard) cuts across the middle of the picture. Most parcels of land were used to farm lemons, Valencia oranges, and walnuts. Balboa Boulevard and Amestoy Avenue frame the picture vertically. The new Encino Reservoir, in the Santa Monica Mountains, is visible at the top right.

The city of Encino is beginning to take shape in this aerial shot that shows the State Highway (Ventura Boulevard) bisecting the middle of the picture. The pear-shaped lake of the rancho is seen in the center of the photograph. On the left, the vertical rectangle of trees and grass above the highway is Encino Park. Above the rectangle is the site of the Encino Elementary School, constructed in 1923.

The above photograph, taken on July 21, 1921, shows the home of Jerome B. and Mary Desnoyers at 17150 State Highway. The back of the photograph states that the Desnoyers family traveled to the Van Nuys Post Office to receive their mail. At the time, there was no postal service to then-rural Encino. A beautiful oak tree, always a dominant presence in Encino, stands in their front yard above. The Desnoyers loved their new custom-built home, which cost around $7,000. Their sunny dining room, seen in the photograph below, was equipped with electric lighting.

In the above photograph, 83-year-old J. B. Desnoyers stands proudly beside his newly planted walnut grove. Desnoyers kept busy on his property growing and harvesting a variety of produce. J. B. and Mary Desnoyers were typical of other Easterners who came to California in their retirement years. They lived with their son, Victor E., who built an adjoining house on the property. The couple celebrated their 60th wedding anniversary on July 12, 1925. According to a newspaper account of the occasion, after 60 years of marriage, Jerome and Mary were still in love with each other. He stated that he always met his wife at breakfast with a kiss, and she said she always received her man as a beau when he returned from a trip to the city. They both passed away, only days apart, in 1935.

The Encino Country Club opened in 1923 and was designed with the whole family in mind. The 1,820-acre estate was located at the original end of Havenhurst Avenue, at the base of the mountains. It boasted many different kinds of sports facilities, including golf, swimming, tennis, bowling-on-the-green, croquet, canoeing, trap shooting, and a 1,000-yard rifle range, as well as horseback riding, with many miles of trails. The club built an extension to Havenhurst Avenue to enable its guests to travel over the Santa Monica Mountains to the beach. The country club closed 10 years later as a result of bankruptcy during the Great Depression. The property was taken over by the Raenford Military School and then was finally torn down for the Earl White subdivision. (Courtesy of USC Special Collections.)

This postcard shows the home of famous movie star Mickey Rooney. He once lived at 4723 White Oak Avenue with his parents. The residence had been the former home of Spencer Tracy. Other celebrities who have lived in Encino at one time or another are Michael Jackson, John Wayne, Cybill Shepherd, and Ron Howard.

Newlyweds Clark Gable and Carole Lombard also made their home, shown here on another postcard, in an elaborate farmhouse in rural Encino at 4543 Tara Drive, in the hills just south of the Ventura Highway. There the couple, who called each other Ma and Pa, raised horses, dogs, and chickens. The house is now gone and has been replaced by an exclusive subdivision.

The Sepulveda Boulevard Tunnel, at the edge of the southern border of Encino, cut 655 feet beneath the Santa Monica Mountains and linked the San Fernando Valley and West Los Angeles. The formal dedication was celebrated on September 27, 1930, as a caravan of 100 automobiles and horsemen, dressed in Spanish costumes, made its way up the mountain from Ventura Boulevard. The new tunnel costs over $500,000, but it saved motorists 12 miles of travel when making the journey. (Courtesy of USC Special Collections.)

The de la Ossa Adobe obtained historic monument status during this 1937 dedication ceremony led by Marie Welsh Harrington and the Native Daughters of the Golden West. Peter Amestoy, the third person from the left, watches with his arms folded. Standing behind Peter is another Basque, longtime family friend Los Angeles sheriff Eugene Biscailuz.

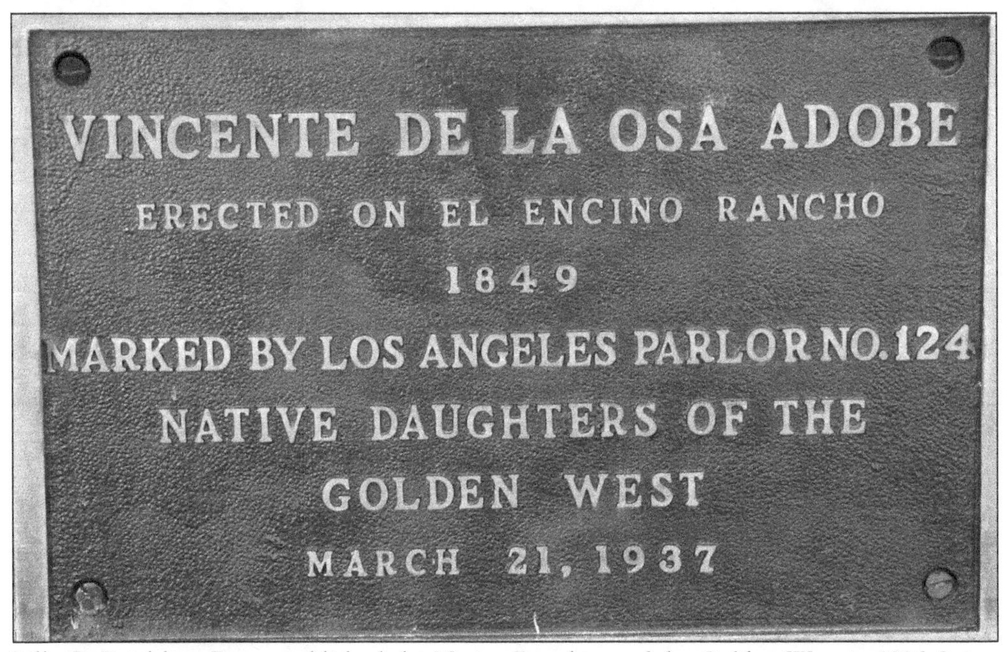

Lilly O. Reichling Dyer established the Native Daughters of the Golden West in 1886. It is a fraternal and patriotic organization for all native Californians. Marie Walsh Harrington was the wife of Dr. Mark Harrington, the director of the Southwest Museum. He was responsible for restoring the Andres Pico Adobe in San Fernando. Marie Harrington was active in preserving historic landmarks of Southern California. (Photograph by the author.)

A few notable early Encino residents pose at the northern end of the de la Ossa Adobe. Constant Gless, a son of Simon Gless, is the fourth from the left, and Peter Amestoy, his uncle, stands at the bottom of the steps. The young actor Don Ameche sits on a white horse. The Native Daughters of the Golden West plaque is visible on the adobe wall.

Encino finally got its own post office, located in a corner of the Encino Store. On hand for the April 18, 1938, dedication is actor Arthur Treacher, standing on the far left. To the right of Treacher are Peter Amestoy, a partially hidden Don Ameche, and Elizabeth Amestoy Wells. The new postmaster and store owner, Ted Gibson, appears in the window wearing the white shirt, while Edward Everett Horton hams it up on the right. Honorary Encino mayor Al Jolson, in the light-colored suit holding his hat, grins for the camera.

Ted Gibson, Encino's first postmaster, was not only the mailman but also a friend of the many movie stars who lived in the area. Born in Texas, Gibson came to California at the age of seven. His store/gas station on Ventura Boulevard, near Oak Park Avenue, was a favorite meeting place. He is quoted, in an oral history interview conducted by the author in the early 1990s, as saying, "I was running a grocery and service station so it was the only spot, regardless of politics." Shirley Gibson, Ted's daughter, received the first letter (also the first registered letter ever delivered to Encino) on opening day, April 18, 1938 (below). While her mail was close at hand, she still had to travel to high school in Van Nuys.

The Army Corps of Engineers purchased the lower southeastern end of the rancho in the early 1900s and held it as the Sepulveda Flood Control Basin. After the devastating storm and flood of February and March 1938, the corps completed the dam on December 30, 1941, in order to control sporadic winter floods along the Los Angeles River. The iconic Sepulveda Dam is an impervious, rolled-earth embankment with a reinforced concrete spillway. Its crest length is 2.93 miles long. The maximum height above the original Los Angeles River streambed is 57 feet. The dramatic sight of the dam was hidden from the public until the freeway system, built in the 1950s, provided elevation high enough to see it. It is one of the most famous structures in the San Fernando Valley. (Both photographs by the author.)

The mound at the ranch had been a characteristic feature beside the Encino lake. It can be seen in many historic photographs, but there is no trace of it today. When the valley became more populated, and as more of the ranch was parceled out, the mound was in the way of progress. In the late 1930s, the two-lane State Highway needed widening. The mound was leveled, and the dirt was spread out. Various accounts have stated that in the days before the leveling, people drove up in pickup trucks and carried away numerous Native American artifacts. The rolling hills around the rancho were rumored to have been the site of buried treasure.

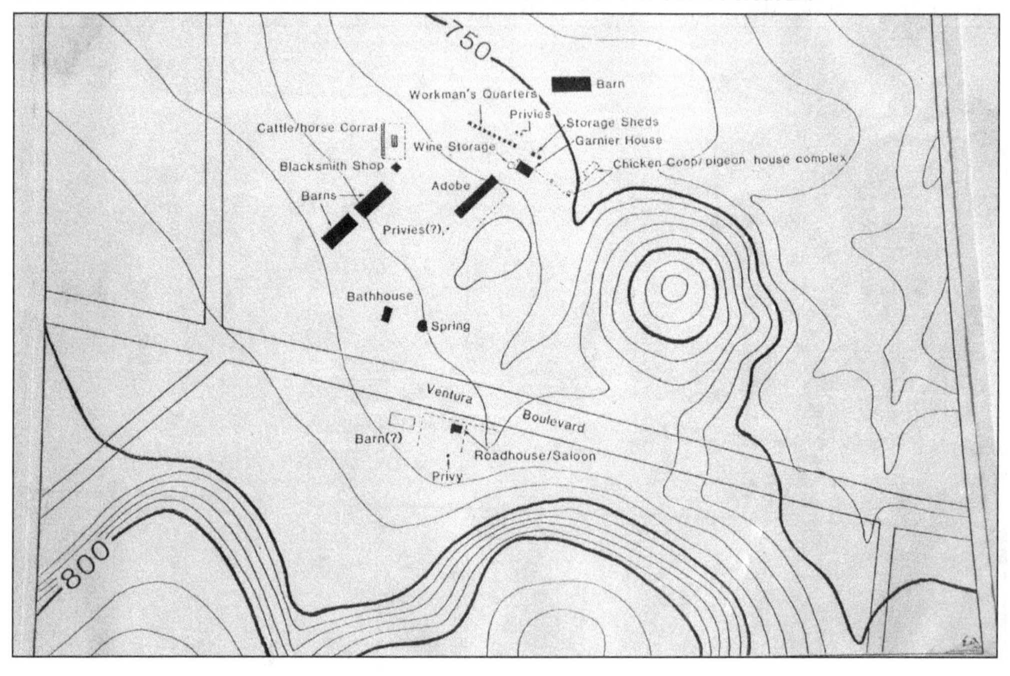

In this picture from 1939, the newly widened Ventura Boulevard is visible. The old restaurant extension, from the 1920s, can be seen on the Garnier Building. Much of Encino was still rural at this time, with lots of open land. Most of the dirt from the mound was spread out across the boulevard, covering the foundation of the old tavern that had burned down in 1906.

By 1944, new buildings stood at the southeast corner of Ventura Boulevard and Genesta Avenue, across the street from the city park. A larger post office had replaced the one in the corner of Ted Gibson's old Encino Store. The Red Cross also set up shop during World War II, and a new drugstore/soda fountain opened for business. (Courtesy of Marc Wanamaker, Bison Productions.)

Another view of the Ventura and Genesta Avenue corner, in 1944, shows a different vantage point of Encino Drugs. The photographs on this page were probably taken minutes apart. Much of the surrounding area was still open land. While the building facade still stands today, the drugstore and Green Lantern Ice Cream are no longer there. (Courtesy of Marc Wanamaker, Bison Productions.)

This 1944 photograph shows the new Encino Post Office building. The building facade still stands today, with its arched window transoms and tiles. The current occupant of the building, at 16946 Ventura Boulevard, is a dry cleaner. At the end of World War II, the San Fernando Valley began to grow at a tremendous rate. Eventually a new, larger post office facility was built on White Oak Avenue. (Courtesy of Marc Wanamaker, Bison Productions.)

This Mayfair Market was located at 5767 White Oak Avenue, the present site of the post office. The Mayfair Company had owned six supermarkets in Los Angeles when it purchased the Van's Markets in 1948. The Encino market was the 20th market in the Mayfair chain, and the sixth store to open in the valley, on October 5, 1950. (Courtesy of Marc Wanamaker, Bison Productions.)

The Monty's Steak House sign is partially visible in this photograph of Ventura Boulevard looking west in 1974. Monty Levine and his sons owned this family-run business. Monty, an ex-boxer who sold liquor to restaurants from his truck, became the owner of a restaurant when the restaurant owed him money. He managed the first restaurant in Pasadena. His son Larry and his wife, Bobbi, opened the Encino location at 17016 Ventura Boulevard in 1956. Monty's other son, Dennis, managed the restaurant in Westwood. The only surviving Monty's Restaurant is in Woodland Hills and is operated by Larry's son, Michael, the inventor of the butterfly corkscrew. (Courtesy of Marc Wanamaker, Bison Productions.)

Six

The Movies Come to Encino

During the 1920s, the Amestoy Estate Company rented out the Garnier Building for the use as a restaurant. A covered porch was added along with a doorway on the second floor. The restaurant was popular during Prohibition because it operated as a speakeasy and served alcohol. The police raided the restaurant several times, which forced it to close. One story handed down tells that the 14 small rooms on the second floor, once used as bedrooms for the ranch workers, were used as a brothel. In the 1930s, the old restaurant was occasionally used as a location for movies.

This early photograph shows the RKO (Radio-Keith-Orpheum) Encino Ranch on January 1, 1930. The long dirt road running from left to right is what will become Burbank Boulevard. The road on the extreme right is Amestoy Avenue. The main street of the Western town set can be seen in this Spence Airplane photograph. (Courtesy of Marc Wanamaker, Bison Productions.)

This photograph, looking north, shows the *Cimarron* set in 1931. The first Western to win an Oscar, the film received excellent critical reviews, but its initial financial failure was blamed on its being released during one of the darkest periods of the Great Depression. The land-rush scene took a week to film, using 5,000 extras, 28 cameramen, and 27 camera assistants. (Courtesy of Marc Wanamaker, Bison Productions.)

This photograph offers another view of the RKO Ranch looking west toward the town of Marian (Reseda) in 1931. The Los Angeles River snakes up from the bottom center of the picture. The long, white buildings on the right side of the river are part of the Encino railroad station. The second road from the bottom on the right is Balboa Boulevard, and above it is Louise Avenue. (Courtesy of Marc Wanamaker, Bison Productions.)

This 1934 Spence photograph shows one of the farms northwest of Encino. The RKO Ranch can be seen in the upper right-hand corner. The Vanowen Bridge is visible in the middle of the photograph as it spans the Los Angeles River. White Oak Avenue cuts across the center, from left to right. (Courtesy of Marc Wanamaker, Bison Productions.)

This photograph may look like Paris, France, during the Middle Ages, but it is, in reality, the 1939 movie set for *The Hunchback of Notre Dame* in Encino on the RKO Ranch. The set shows the scene where Quasimodo rescues Esmerelda from the noose. The classic film starred Charles Laughton and Maureen O'Hara and was directed by Robert Wise. (Courtesy of Marc Wanamaker, Bison Productions.)

This 1941 photograph of the RKO Ranch looks southeast toward the Sepulveda Dam. The RKO Ranch covered 110 acres that included a street of medieval Paris, a Western street, an airplane hangar, and a New York street, as well as the mansion used in the movie *The Magnificent Ambersons.* (Courtesy of Marc Wanamaker, Bison Productions.)

These two views of the main gate, during the last days of the RKO Ranch, show the corner of Louise Avenue and Burbank Boulevard. The most memorable movie filmed at the ranch was *It's a Wonderful Life*, starring James Stewart and Donna Reed. It was filmed on a hot day in 1946, and the prop department powdered the Encino oaks with white plaster for the winter scenes at the climax of the movie. Cowboy actor Tim Holt made many Westerns at the RKO Ranch. (Both courtesy of Marc Wanamaker, Bison Productions.)

This photograph, taken in the 1940s, shows the large facility of Birmingham General Hospital. Balboa Boulevard is on the left, intersected by Vanowen and Victory Boulevards. Built in Van Nuys, just at the northern edge of Encino, in early 1944, it was named for Gen. Henry Birmingham. The hospital was transferred to the Veterans Administration in 1946 and renamed Birmingham Veteran's Hospital. Visible just beyond the Los Angeles River is RKO Ranch, with the city of Encino in the background. (Courtesy of Marc Wanamaker, Bison Productions.)

In 1950, the community of Encino began crowding the RKO Ranch. There were still houses mixed in with the orchards, but a new housing tract was built on both sides of White Oak Avenue. Van Nuys Airport can be seen in the upper right-hand corner. The Veterans Administration closed the hospital in 1950. The property was converted into use for public schools. It is the current location of Birmingham High School and a middle school. There is no public high school within the actual city limits of Encino. Public school students living in Encino attend either Birmingham or Reseda High School. (Courtesy of Marc Wanamaker, Bison Productions.)

The movie making at the RKO Ranch, in 1952, was beginning to come to a close. Howard Hughes had purchased a controlling interest in RKO in 1948. However, after a series of flops, Hughes began selling off portions of the studio, and he sold the ranch in 1953. (Courtesy of Marc Wanamaker, Bison Productions.)

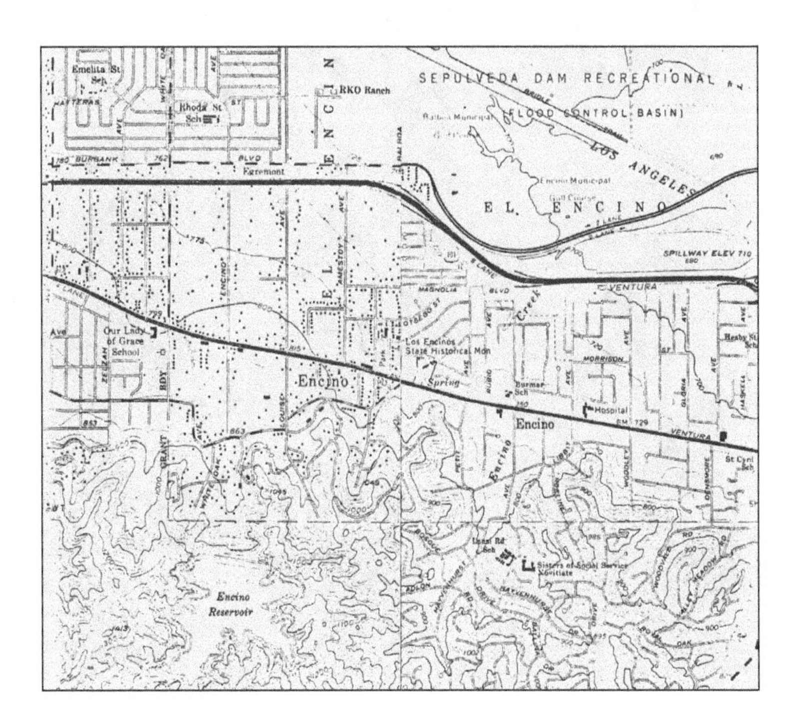

This map from the 1950s still shows the RKO Ranch in the upper center of the picture. The newly built Ventura Freeway separated it from Encino. More schools and churches were also built. The map shows Lanai Road Elementary and Encino Elementary School, in addition to Our Lady of Grace Catholic Church and Crespi Carmelite School on the west end of Encino and St. Cyril of Jerusalem School on the east.

Movie making in Encino may have ended after the demise of the RKO Ranch. However, in 1981, the television series *Lou Grant* brought their trucks and lighting equipment to Los Encino State Historic Park and filmed an episode called "Double Cross" during its fifth season. The plot revolved around the young female reporter on the show, Billie (played by Linda Kelsey), as she worked with a local historian to discover the truth about a valuable gold cross retrieved from a time capsule. The cross became a pawn in a game between two feuding families.

Seven

The End of an Era

Movie director Clarence Brown purchased the remaining acres of the Amestoy Ranch in 1945. His most acclaimed film was *Anna Karenina* with Greta Garbo. Brown kept the run-down rancho for a short time and then sold it to a building syndicate that further subdivided the land. It was during these years that plans were in the works to destroy the historic structures and fill the lake.

The next series of photographs were taken in 1949, after the State of California, Department of Parks and Recreation, had secured the property. The old buildings on the last 4 acres had fallen into considerable disrepair. The last room of the adobe, on the southern end, had been used for a time as a real estate office. Weeds began to take over the property, and Encino residents complained about the vagrants who often lit fires in the abandoned rooms.

These photographs show the dilapidated condition of the nearly 100-year-old adobe. Windows and doors were broken and in pieces on the ground. An old electrical panel was broken and neglected. The doors were boarded up in order to keep out the "bindle bums" (as vagrants were called in those days). The plaster on the adobe walls was very thin and on the verge of exposing the mud bricks to the elements. It was just a little over 10 years earlier that the Daughters of the Golden West had celebrated this historical monument.

The old Garnier restaurant from the 1920s was also falling apart. Holes in the roof and broken windows allowed birds to roost in the second floor. The floorboards on the first floor were broken and uneven. The paint on the walls was curled up like ghostly potato chips. Broken glass and pieces of wood were scattered on the ground. The local children said that the old two-story limestone building looked "spooky." The largely abandoned property was a dangerous place to play.

Sunlight shines through the roof of the old restaurant porch as weeds take over the grounds (right). Visible behind the two-story building is the double-roofed food storage building and corrugated metal lean-to that had been built by the Amestoys and had served as an outdoor pantry for the farm. The unusual double roof helped keep vegetables and sacks of grain cool in the hot summer sun. Shown below, the structures stand open and rusted.

The picturesque photograph above was taken by the State of California in 1949 and shows the 100-year-old de la Ossa Adobe ranch house and the 74-year-old Garnier Building. From a distance, the buildings capture an image of a time from long ago. The many historical stories of the Native Americans, Spanish explorers, French sheepherders, and Basque farmers were slowly fading away as the flood of newcomers streamed into the San Fernando Valley in search of the American dream of owning a home. Land sub-dividers looked at the falling-down rancho buildings as obstacles to the progress of the development of Los Angeles.

Vi Strom, an Encino housewife, gathers warm spring water (above) as it pours out of the spigot from the wall of the springhouse in another publicity photograph from 1949. The "hot" springs were actually a warm 80 degrees. When the state ordered a chemical analysis of the water, they found that the deep artesian spring was free of alkali. The report (below) stated that the water was beneficial to those suffering from acidity of the stomach or acidity of the blood.

ENCINO HOT SPRINGS WATER.

The following analysis of the waters from this Spring is given by Smith Emery Co., Chemists, Los Angeles, Cal.

	Incrusting Solids Grains per gallon
Silica	.82
Calcium Carbonate	.23
Total	1.05
	Non-incrusting Solids
Sodium Carbonate	21.70
Sodium Sulphate	36.60
Sodium Chloride	3.18
Volatile and Organic Matter	5.85
Total	67.33

This water is free from Alkali and is beneficial to those suffering from acidity of the stomach, or acidity of the blood, which causes rheumatism.

Encino Hot Springs

Several local boys are shown taking advantage of the warm waters of the limestone-lined lake, fed by the spring, in this 1949 photograph of the ranch property. The State of California later installed a fence around the lake after one boy drowned. Open space still stretched down to Petit Avenue, and the Sepulveda Pass can be seen in the distance.

Marie Stewart is pictured here with Joseph Amestoy, who offered a donation to help restore Los Encinos. Stewart was an Encino housewife who had met Francoise Amestoy, who gave her a tour of the run-down adobe. Marie Stewart fell in love with the romance of old California, and, according to an oral history conducted by the author in the early 1990s, she had decided, at the time, to take it upon herself to "do battle with land developers . . . and endure political red tape" to save the buildings.

Edward Everett Horton was a significant supporter of Encino and the Encino Historical Society. The longtime resident offered his "barn" for numerous fund-raising dances in the days following the end of World War II. He is best known to the public as the sidekick of Fred Astaire in the movie *Top Hat*, and in 1959, he narrated the *Rocky and Bullwinkle Show*'s animated cartoon segment called *Fractured Fairy Tales*. In 1965, he played the medicine man Roaring Chicken in the television situation comedy *F Troop*. Horton's home was eventually torn down to make way for the Ventura Freeway. A short extension of Amestoy Avenue was renamed Edward Everett Horton Lane in his honor. He died in 1970 at the age of 86. (Below, photograph by Amy Goldenberg.)

The Native Daughters of the Golden West rededicated the adobe with a second plaque after Marie Stewart and the Encino Historical Society fought to save the old buildings on the ranch from demolition. It is interesting to note that the original plaque from 1937 referred to the adobe builder as Vincente. After Stewart conducted research, she discovered that his first name was actually Vicente. There are also two different spellings of his last name. Early Los Angeles documents show that his name spelled both Osa and Ossa. The current family spelling favors the form de la Ossa.

Local photographer Cal Turner shot a series of photographs in 1970 that were donated to the park for archive purposes. These pictures show the Garnier Building after the state had dismantled the broken restaurant porch. Holes along the base of the second story (right) show where the roof of the porch attached to the building. The door on the second floor is visible. A new roof had also been added. Unfortunately, following the 1971 Sylmar earthquake, the structure was determined to be unsafe. The state also removed the stairway that led to the second-floor landing for safety (below). Pieces of the limestone blocks are visible between the two back doors. (Both courtesy of Cal Turner.)

Marie Stewart poses for Cal Turner in the Amestoy Parlor (left), a re-created room display in the de la Ossa Adobe at the time he took the photographs. Stewart had spent several decades contacting family members of past owners of the property and researching information about the history of the rancho. Portraits of Francoise and Jean-Baptiste Amestoy hang on the wall behind her as she sits on a horsehair sofa, one of the many donated family heirlooms she was able to obtain for the adobe room displays. She remarked in her oral history interview with the author that the fight to save the property and its buildings was enormous. Over two years, "each step of progress was followed with disheartening setbacks."

From left to right, Marie Stewart, Lois Carr, and Constance Bennett sit for a portrait next to the antique dresser donated to the park by the de la Ossa family. Many of the ladies of the historical society loved to dress in Spanish costumes during their open house celebrations. Many of the local historical sites were saved from demolition because of the hard work and dedication of women like Marie Stewart and her colleagues.

The state wanted to install a public restroom on the park property in the 1980s. Construction was halted when workers unearthed this unusual limestone pad. Originally, historians believed it was the remnants of a long-lost wing of the adobe, but no other remains were ever found. This photograph shows an archaeologist observing a dime dating to 1872. A public restroom was eventually built 25 feet from this spot. Today the limestone pad can be seen, surrounded by a wooden fence, on the site of Los Encinos State Historic Park.

Restoration and earthquake retrofitting of the Garnier Building began in 1988. In 1991, the park celebrated the reopening of the Garnier Building. Docent president Michael Crosby, on the steps, stands with a representative of then state senator Alan Robbins (left) and California State Park district superintendent Susan Ross (right). The Fort Tejon Civil War Band plays. After years of research and work, the old dining room on the first floor became a visitors center. Jean Bischoff, a former docent president, is shown taping the proceedings from the visitors center's window.

The Garnier Building underwent many changes over the years. State historians discovered the interior had been remodeled three times since it was built in 1872. The door on the right side originally led to the kitchen. The door on the left led to a dining room. A large dance floor surface was also uncovered, probably used during its years as a restaurant/speakeasy.

Eight

THE SEPULVEDA DAM

In this photograph from April 12, 1951, Lt. Col. W. R. Shuler, head of the Army Corps of Engineers, points to a map that details the new plan for the Sepulveda Dam Recreation Area. Also on hand for this publicity photograph is Los Angeles mayor Fletcher Bowron (standing front left); George Hjelte, general manager of the city Recreation and Parks Commission (standing in the back); and Robert Burns (in the double-breasted suit), president of the Recreation and Parks Commission. (Courtesy of USC Special Collections.)

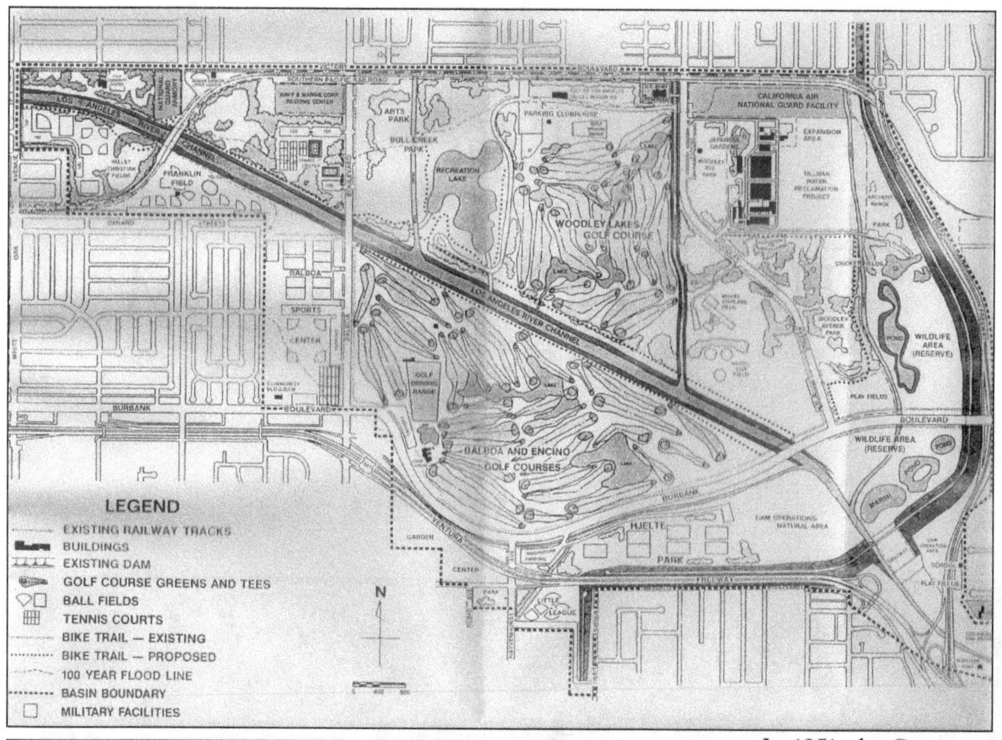

In 1951, the City of Los Angeles acquired a 50-year lease for 1,700 acres in the northeastern section of what had once been a part of the old Encino Rancho and built the Sepulveda Dam Recreation Area. One of the largest open spaces in the San Fernando Valley, it features several large recreation areas, including parks, three golf courses, a model aircraft field, an Olympic velodrome, a Japanese garden, a wildlife refuge, a water reclamation plant, and an armory. (Both courtesy of U.S. Army Corps of Engineers, Los Angeles District.)

In these two photographs, taken behind the soccer fields at the recreation area, the natural flow of the Los Angeles River enters a new channel that leads into the park. The source of the river comes from runoff from the merger of the Chatsworth and Bell Creeks, at the base of the Simi Hills to the northwest. Early maps mistakenly show the source of the river to be in Encino because the water table of the San Fernando Valley is lowest in that area. (Both photographs by the author.)

Balboa Sports Center occupies the western part of the large Sepulveda Basin Complex. The indoor facility sports a large gym, two club rooms, and kitchen facilities. Outdoors there are 16 lighted tennis courts, 4 lighted baseball diamonds, 2 lighted basketball courts, and 13 unlighted soccer fields (above), as well as handball and volleyball courts. Across Balboa Boulevard from the center, visitors will find Lake Balboa (below), located within Anthony C. Beilenson Park, an 80-acre recreational facility within the Sepulveda Flood Control basin. The man-made lake is 27 acres and is filled with water reclaimed from the nearby Tillman Water Reclamation Plant. Activities to enjoy in this area include fishing, boating, remote-controlled boating, jogging, and walking, in addition to several play areas with climbing structures and slides for children. (Above, photograph by Michael Crosby; below, photograph by Amy Goldenberg.)

The Donald C. Tillman Water Reclamation Plant, named after the city engineer who conceived and developed the entire complex, is located on a 90-acre site leased to the city by the U.S. Army Corps of Engineers for 50 years at a nominal cost of $100 per acre per year. Tillman devised this unique way to use treated sewer water. (Photograph by Amy Goldenberg.)

The reclamation project of the Los Angeles City Department of Public Works is funded by grants from the Environmental Protection Agency and the State Water Resources Control Board, as well as by funds from the city's Sewer Construction and Maintenance Fund. Water treated through the plant fills the Wildlife Nature Reserve, Lake Balboa, and the lake next to the Japanese garden (above), and it is used in the Sepulveda sprinkler system. The reclamation process is completed every 11.5 hours and generates 65 million gallons of reclaimed water per day. Dr. Koichi Kawana created the Japanese garden (below). Eventually the water enters the Los Angeles River. (Both photographs by Amy Goldenberg.)

Community activists and government planners developed the idea for a designated wildlife reserve in the 1960s and 1970s, when much of the basin was still open land but was becoming surrounded by suburban growth. Citizens thought it critical to preserve land in the lowest flood-prone basin areas and re-create a natural habitat for birds and small animals with native vegetation where the community would be welcome as visitors. Sepulveda Basin Wildlife Area is the result. The area provides a safe open place for migrating flocks and birdwatchers alike. A system of walking trails was also created in wooded areas north and south of Burbank Boulevard. (Above, photograph by Amy Goldenberg; below, photograph by Michael Crosby.)

San Vicente Mountain Park overlooks Encino and the rest of the San Fernando Valley from the top of the Santa Monica Mountains. From 1956 to 1968, San Vicente Mountain was one of 16 Los Angeles–area Nike-Ajax anti-aircraft missile launch sites. The site contained ground-based radar designed to detect hostile aircraft during the cold war. The original radar tower, pictured here, offers spectacular views of the 20,000-acre wilderness parks. (Photograph by the author.)

Encino Reservoir is located on the site of what was, originally, Encino Creek. Construction of the reservoir was completed in 1924. Its normal surface area is 158 acres. It serves as one of four reservoirs in the San Fernando Valley, along with Hanson Dam, Chatsworth Reservoir, and the Van Norman Dam. (Photograph by the author.)

Nine

Forces of Nature

Seen here is the famous Encino oak tree, also known as the Lang Oak. It was a California live oak, *Quercus agrifolia.* The oak tree became a local landmark because of its size and longevity. Its age was determined to be 1,000 years, and it was considered to be the oldest tree in the city of Los Angeles. Encino itself is named for the Spanish word for "oak." The Encino oak was the most magnificent of the community's many oaks. It was so large that Louise Avenue, on the south side of Ventura Boulevard, was split to accommodate its enormous 150-foot canopy. Its likeness is portrayed on the Encino Chamber of Commerce logo.

Construction was stopped at the Ventura Boulevard location of the First Financial Group office complex in December 1980 when the foundation of the old tavern/stagecoach stop built by the Garnier Brothers in the 1870s was unearthed. Behind the foundation, the archaeologists discovered a trash pit to the rear of the main structure, considered a gold mine to archeologists. Teams of archaeologists combed the area, collecting and cataloging over a million artifacts, such as bottles, plates, and hundreds of sheep bones. Some artifacts from this dig are displayed at Los Encinos State Park in the visitors center.

A closer inspection of the surroundings unearthed the remains of several Native Americans. Leaders from three Native American tribes said that the excavation desecrated the graves of their ancestors. They demanded that the remains be reburied. Local tribal members and state officials decided they would secretly return the remains across the street to the historic park late at night. It is very likely that some of what was found during this dig had been pushed to the location when the ancient mound (discussed on page 64) was leveled in the 1930s.

By the 1990s, the famous oak tree was in a weakened condition. It suffered from oak-root fungus or "slime flux," a tree ailment caused by a bacteria that generates fermentation inside the tree and sends toxic sap oozing through the bark. On February 7, 1998, a storm delivered the death blow, felling the ailing tree with storm winds. As news of the tree's demise spread, onlookers gathered, some crying and taking branches as mementos. As souvenir-hunters sought to take pieces of the tree, police officers guarded it until its remains could be removed. One officer noted, "It got out of control. It's sad that we had to take two policemen off the street to watch a tree."

In 1958, the oak tree's standing in the community had been threatened when a developer planned to bulldoze it to build a road, what is now Louise Avenue. Local residents formed a group called Encino Save the Oaks, and the developer eventually donated the tree to the city. Ultimately, the road was split around the tree. The oak tree was designated Los Angeles Historic Cultural Monument No. 24 in 1963. All that is left of the oak tree is the 8-by-6-foot oval stump pictured above. After it fell, the city opted to plant five new trees on the site of the famous oak, three California sycamores and two coast live oaks. The trees were dedicated in a ribbon-cutting ceremony in April 1999. They can be seen today along with this historic maker on the south side of Ventura Boulevard on Louise Avenue.

At 4:30 a.m. on January 17, 1994, the magnitude 6.7 Northridge earthquake awakened residents of the greater Los Angeles area and beyond. The quake caused more than 50 deaths, left over 20,000 homeless, and resulted in estimated damages of over $15 billion. All of the historic structures at Los Encinos State Historic Park were extensively damaged, including the de la Ossa Adobe. The entire end wall collapsed, leaving the interior fully exposed to the elements.

Many of the museum objects that had been on exhibit in the adobe were covered with dust and fragments of adobe plaster. Following the earthquake, extensive investigations of the adobe provided a wealth of information, including evidence of previous earthquake repairs, such as the large crack uncovered from under the fallen plaster above the door in one of the interior bedrooms. In another bedroom, fallen plaster lays on top of an antique bed.

Photographs taken on January 17, 1994, show other views of the serious damage. The photograph above shows a view of the northern end of the adobe; a large chunk of the structure looks bitten off. The photograph below shows a wide gash on the wall next to the door. Evidence of past earthquake repairs was found in the cracks. When the 1769 Portola/Crespi Spanish expedition arrived in Los Angeles, prior to leaving for the San Fernando Valley, they reported experiencing severe earthquakes. Other severe earthquakes occurred in the area in 1812, 1855, 1856, and the Tejon earthquake in 1857.

The Garnier Building also suffered from the Northridge earthquake. The main reason the structure did not crumble to the ground on January 17, 1994, was because of the retrofitting completed three years before and celebrated with the opening of the visitors center. The vertical steel beam (right) can be seen in front of the hole between the two windows on the first floor. The sight of the building above caused one docent of the park to remark after seeing the damage, "It looks like the building is smiling because it is still standing."

The blacksmith shop at Los Encinos State Historic Park suffered only minor damage. It was the first building to be repaired and reopened after the earthquake. All the structures were fenced off for six years, some longer, as engineers, architects, and conservators put all the pieces back together. Special epoxy was injected between the blocks and stones of every building for future protection. Currently, one room in the adobe displays the actual state of the interior following the 1994 Northridge earthquake. The walls were left bare to expose the inner structure. An audio-visual presentation can be viewed that shows actual footage of the variety of preservation-related efforts made after the earthquake.

As the state conservator began replacing the plaster fragments in the Garnier salon room of the adobe after the earthquake, she discovered a tiny flash of color under the many layers of paint. This surprising find caused her to call in an expert to carefully remove the many layers of paint. Surprisingly, individual painted panels, decorated in a style popular in France from the 1840s to 1870s, were revealed. The long vertical panels, each one with a faux-frame border, were painted to look like marble. Archeologists date the treatment to the period when the Garniers remodeled the entire ranch. The rest of this adobe room depicts a French salon, as the Garnier family may have kept it during their residence at the rancho (1868–1878). Because of the dedicated work of the state conservators on this project, Los Encinos State Historic Park won the 2008 Governor's Award for their contribution to the "reinterpretation of California history."

In 2007, the de la Ossa Adobe finally reopened to the public, the last of the structures at Los Encinos State Historic Park to be restored after the 1994 earthquake. In all, it had taken over 13 years of hard work and planning to bring Encino's oldest buildings back from the edge of disaster. The old adobe and the other buildings at the park are a testament not only to the rich history of California but also the will to survive, demonstrated through the efforts of many people over time to build, alter, save, and preserve Rancho El Encino.

Ten

Encino Today

The Encino Village was built on the former site of the RKO Ranch. In June 1955, a total of 233 three- or four-bedroom homes were priced from $15,600 to $16,625. Each of the nine different floor plans in the development had two bathrooms and two-car garages. Homes were offered to veterans with no down payment. At one time, a large shopping center was planned for the ex–RKO Ranch site. (Photograph by Amy Goldenberg.)

The original Encino Elementary School building was constructed in 1923 on Encino Acres land dedicated by W. H. Hay. Today's buildings date back to the late 1950s. (Photograph by the author.)

Lanai Road Elementary School was constructed in 1959, and it serves a student body of approximately 500 in grades kindergarten through fifth. Lanai Road Elementary School serves both local students and students who travel from outside of Encino. (Photograph by the author.)

St. Nicholas' Episcopal Church, on Ventura Boulevard, was dedicated on January 8, 1939, the San Fernando Valley's first Episcopal congregation. The original 1939 design is in the California mission style. The Great Bronze Doors, the work of Henry Van Wolf, were dedicated in 1957. Los Encinos School is a private school affiliated with the church. (Photograph by the author.)

Holy Martyrs Armenian Apostolic Church was established in 1959. The Holy Martyrs Armenian Elementary and Ferrahian High School, located on White Oak Avenue, was the first Armenian Day School in the United States. The school opened its doors in September 1964 with a student body of 12. (Photograph by the author.)

Los Angeles mayor Sam Yorty was a guest of honor at the ground-breaking ceremonies in 1963 for the new sanctuary, social hall, and religious school for Valley Beth Shalom, a Conservative congregation on Ventura Boulevard, close to the east end of Encino. The cornerstone for the new building was quarried on Mount Zion, in Israel, and shipped to Los Angeles. The inscription on the cornerstone reads, "And in this place I give you peace." The formal opening dedication was held on June 10, 1966. (Photograph by the author.)

St. Cyril of Jerusalem School was founded in 1949. The name comes from the fourth-century bishop of Jerusalem. Timothy Cardinal Manning gave the name to the new parish in the valley to show concern for holy sites in the State of Israel following its year of independence. The school serves children in preschool through the eighth grade. (Photograph by the author.)

Our Lady of Grace Parish and Elementary School, for preschool through eighth-grade students, developed over 50 years at its location at 5011 White Oak Avenue. The church celebrated its first mass on December 16, 1945, in the packing room of Canoga Farms, owned by Frank Flowers, a Presbyterian. Crespi Carmelite High School, located on the south side of the church, was established in Encino in 1959. (Photograph by the author.)

The First Presbyterian Church of Encino sanctuary was built in 1954 and underwent a major redesign in 2002. The original design was traditional 1950s ecclesiastical architecture, with the clergy and choir separated from the congregation. The new interior design (not shown) is more open and inclusive. It has been awarded honors by local, state, and national branches of the American Institute of Architects for interior design. (Photograph by the author.)

The Bethel Lutheran Church purchased 2.5 acres of land in Encino in March 1951. The property, on the corner of Burbank Boulevard and Encino Avenue, originally consisted of a three-bedroom house, a swimming pool, and a small citrus grove. They became known as "the church with a swimming pool." Their first pastor, Frederick J. Schenk, was chosen by the Mission Department of the Evangelical Lutheran Church in 1951. Bethel Lutheran Church was named by Pastor Schenk in honor of his hometown church in Madison, Wisconsin. (Photograph by the author.)

The Sisters of Social Service of Los Angeles, a Catholic women's religious community in the 1940s, founded Holy Spirit Retreat Center. It was the first retreat center for women in Los Angeles. First located in the mid-Wilshire area, it moved to its current location in 1969. The facility served as a novitiate (training place for new sisters) from 1960 until it became the retreat center. (Photograph by the author.)

The Tapia Brothers have been farming in the San Fernando Valley for three generations. Founded by Primo Tapia, it is one of the last produce stands in the valley. The small farm on Havenhurst Avenue is situated on land that was once part of the Amestoy Ranch. The original Tapia Brothers farm was located where Lake Balboa now sits. In 1984, they bought the present site, formerly the family-owned Maria's Corn Stand, built in the early 1970s. Primo Tapia eventually turned the business over to sons Felix and Charles. Today it is run by Primo's grandsons, Tom and Felix Tapia. They have produced fresh corn and other fine vegetables for years, and it is a great place to take little kids. (Photograph by the author.)

The old Encino Community Building was built in the early 1920s on land donated to the city by Encino Acres developer W. H. Hay. Hay had offered the land for a park and restrooms for the convenience of motorists who traveled the Ventura Highway. The Encino Community Building currently houses the California Traditional Music Society. The park on Ventura Boulevard also includes a toddler playground and basketball and tennis courts. It is often confused with Los Encinos State Historic Park, which is one block away across Balboa Boulevard. (Photograph by the author.)

This 1990s photograph shows Los Encinos State Historic Park's Easter egg hunt on the lawn near the lake. This annual event for children is free to the public. It is an example of one of the traditional activities that were popular during the 19th century in Southern California. Other old-fashioned games, like tug-o-war, graces, and hoops, can be played at the park's monthly Living History program. They demonstrate to people of all ages how children passed the time before the invention of electricity.

Living History performer Dante Fields, shown here on the right as an 1870-era ranch cook named Buster, pontificates to his not-so-helpful friend, Mike Ferand (in the white shirt), at the 1989 Christmas presentation. Buster let the children help him make his grandma's famous Plum Puddin', as long as they could put up with clowning around.

Walter Nelson was the popular president of the Los Encinos Docent Association during the years after tours of the property were moved outside because of the extensive damage to the historic buildings from the 1994 Northridge earthquake. Always the master of many characters, Walter is dressed here as the dapper bachelor and former rancho owner Eugene Garnier.

When the blacksmith shop was repaired after the Northridge earthquake, docent Gary Standke labored hard at restoring the building into a working unit of the Living History program. Gary, his family, and other volunteers come to the park every third Sunday of the month to demonstrate the forgotten art and craft of blacksmithing, which would have been an important skill in the

1870s in the San Fernando Valley. His wife, Nita, also participates in the program with cooking demonstrations, such as baking bread on an open fire outside the shop and churning butter with active involvement from visiting children. (Both photographs by the author.)

The de la Ossa Adobe has survived for 160 years. It has withstood earthquakes, vandals, and the wrecking ball. This old stagecoach stop along El Camino Real sits quietly along busy Ventura Boulevard. It has become a living memorial to the diverse cultures that have always been a part of the San Fernando Valley. Most neighbors pass by the restored structures without noticing the colorful history of Southern California. First visited by the Chumash and Fernandino Indians, then the Spanish explorers, followed by ranching by Californios, French, and Basque settlers, the park is now in the hands of modern-day residents. (Photograph by the author.)

The Springhouse protects the source of Encino's artesian water. In this photograph from 1973, gaps in the weathered plaster expose pieces of the limestone. This ancient flow has borne witness to the great passage of time. Long ago, it rose up from a barren landscape of oak groves and sycamore trees, a welcome rest spot on the harsh semi-arid valley floor. People have always gathered here to relax and work. The acidic water has washed acorns, quenched cattle and sheep, and bathed dusty travelers. It is up to the current residents of Encino to make sure that the waters of Los Encinos remain open for everyone.